The Fiber Fueled Cookbook

Jack E. Eidson

Published by Healthy life Publishing, 2022.

While every precaution has been taken in the preparation of this book, the publisher assumes no responsibility for errors or omissions, or for damages resulting from the use of the information contained herein.

THE FIBER FUELED COOKBOOK

First edition. June 1, 2022.

Copyright © 2022 Jack E. Eidson.

ISBN: 979-8201814533

Written by Jack E. Eidson.

The Fiber Fueled Cookbook:

How to Improve Your Digestive Health by Cooking Delicious Plant-Based Gut Recipes Lose weight, improve your health, and optimize your microbiome easily.

The Fiber Alternative

Our food culture is enamored with "superfoods," as you may have observed. We're all hoping for that one game-changing solution that will solve all of our health issues and make us feel like a million dollars. We're urged to look for medicines that will help us feel better. Maximum outcomes with minimal effort. Don't get me wrong: superfoods (and pharmaceuticals, if necessary) are fantastic. But we got it all mixed up since no cuisine is capable of living up to that standard. There aren't enough plants on the planet for us to choose just one and eat it.

There is no such thing as perfect cuisine; each one has its own set of advantages and disadvantages. It's possible to have too much of a good thing. You would be quite unhealthy if you only ate kale. We miss out on plant diversity when we only focus on superfoods. Superfoods are cool, but I'd rather have plant-based diversity any day of the week.

Keep in mind that food is more than simply a collection of individual components; it's a complete product. Do the advantages outweigh the disadvantages? Bring more positive than bad food into your life. We get the most out of our diet when we do this. That's where plant-based diversity comes in—while no plant is ideal in and of itself, the benefits far exceed the drawbacks, and when taken together, you get a diet that's precisely customized to promote a healthy gut microbiota and overall health.

To get the best of both worlds, we can concentrate on plant diversity while still incorporating foods that are truly nutritional powerhouses. Although these supercharged foods can be our "best friends," they should not be our sole pals.

Here are some of my favorite Fiber Fueled foods, neatly grouped into an acronym for easy recall. These are the foods I attempt to incorporate as often as possible, however they are most effective when eaten in combination with other plant kinds.

F GOALS F: Fermented Fruit

G: Grains and Greens

O: Omega-3 Super Seeds

A: Aromatics (onions, garlic)

L: Legumes

S: Sulforaphane (Sulforaphane) (broccoli sprouts and other cruciferous veggies)

F: Fermented Fruit

Fermented foods were honored for their increased nutritional value, prebiotics, probiotics, and postbiotic enrichment. They also provide us with more plant-based variety in our diet. Keep in mind that the goal is to incorporate a small amount of fermented foods into our everyday routine.

However, there is a second "F" in our F GOALS: fruit. Fruit is feared by many people, especially in the fitness field, where I've seen or heard numerous personal trainers warn, "Fruit has sugar, and much sugar can contribute to weight gain." People, we shouldn't look at food solely through the lens of its constituent components since it will lead us to draw false judgments. We must consider whole foods. Fruit sugar is not at all the same as processed sugar. It's rich with vitamins and minerals, phytochemicals, and fiber, along with everything else in the fruit.

No, eating entire fruit does not make you gain weight. In fact, it's the polar opposite. For that regard, it does not cause diabetes. Instead, it has the ability to defend against it. Berry, for example, despite their sweetness, lowers blood sugar and insulin release after a meal. Don't confuse natural sugar in whole fruit with added or processed sugars, whether you're diabetic or trying to avoid sugar for another reason. You certainly must consume fruit! It can assist you in losing weight and managing your diabetes.

So, while apples and oranges are delicious, let me tell you about my passion for berries: blueberries, blackberries, raspberries, strawberries, and the lesser-known acai and goji berries. Give them all to me!

Berries occur in a rainbow of hues, including blue, purple, red, and pink. Anthocyanins, a phytochemical (remember, "phyto" means "plant-based"), are responsible for the hue. Blueberries would be green if they didn't contain anthocyanins. Because the anthocyanins haven't arrived yet, immature blueberries aren't blue. Anthocyanins are extremely powerful antioxidants. They aid in cancer prevention and cognitive enhancement. Women who ate just two servings of strawberries or one serving of blueberries each week, for example, were able to delay cognitive decline and make their brain act thirty months younger in one study.

Another study found that eating two servings of berries each week reduced the risk of Parkinson's disease by 23%. And when kids were fed wild blueberries, their cognitive function improved nearly immediately, with the dose of blueberries increasing. I recently completed an eight-hour exam to renew my internal medicine board certification. Guess what I ate for the entire day? Blueberries.

But don't overlook the fiber content. There are 3, 4, 8, and 8 grams of fiber in a one-cup serving of strawberries, blueberries, blackberries, and raspberries, respectively. A small handful of berries can make a tremendous difference when the average American only gets 15 or 16 grams of fiber per day. As an afternoon snack or when I have a sweet tooth, I enjoy popping a couple of handfuls of berries.

G: Grains and Greens

We talked about the benefits of whole grains, including a lower risk of coronary heart disease, cardiovascular disease, and overall cancer, as well as a lower chance of death from any cause, including respiratory diseases, infectious diseases, diabetes, and all non-cardiovascular, non-cancer reasons. That was simply one experiment. From my perspective, it's quite straightforward. Definitely skip the refined grains. I completely agree with you. However, if you want a healthy microbiome, whole grains are the foundation of a healthy gut.

Greens are the second most important "G" in the house. Collards, kale, arugula, spinach, romaine, bok choy, watercress, Swiss chard, broccoli raab, mustard greens, sorrel, escarole, kohlrabi, and more are all examples of plant-based diversity. There are other variations within these items. Curly, lacinato (called dinosaur or Tuscan kale), Redbor, and Siberian kale are just a few examples. Even the leaves of certain common root vegetables, such as beet, turnip, dandelion, radish, and carrots, are edible and add to the green variety.

Nutrient density is an important aspect to consider when evaluating the health benefits of food.

The goal is to receive as many nutrients—vitamins, minerals, phytochemicals, and fiber—as possible per calorie consumed. Nutrient density equals nutrients divided by calories becomes a simple formula. So, take oil, for example, which is high in calories but low in nutrients. Nutrient density is low. Alternatively, potato chips. Calories are plentiful, but nutrients are scarce. Isn't this a really basic and sensible approach?

The ANDI score, which stands for Aggregate Nutrient Density Index and was created by Dr. Joel Fuhrman, one of my personal health heroes, is what we call it. The scale runs from one to one thousand, with one being the worst. Cola, corn chips, and vanilla ice cream, for example, received the lowest marks. That seems about correct.

Kale, collards, mustard greens, watercress, and Swiss chard were among the top achievers, with a perfect 1,000 score. The next four top scoring vegetables were bok choy, spinach, arugula, and romaine. Greens were the top nine foods on the list, in other words. This wasn't a list of only green foods. Although all foods were qualified, greens had the upper hand.

GREENS' RIDICULOUSLY high nutritional richness is a gift from Mother Nature. You receive a lot of nutrients for nearly no calories, which means you can eat as much as you want. It's a way to obtain your nutrition without the calories! A pound of leafy greens, for example, contains only 100 calories. That's roughly one egg or two steak bites. Since switching to a plant-based diet, I've stopped thinking about portion sizes, but if you still want to eat high-calorie dishes after reading this book, know that you may add as much greens as you like to acquire additional nutrients without sacrificing calories.

Let's look at a few examples of nutritional density in action:

Kale includes the antioxidant phytochemicals lutein and zeaxanthin, which the eyes need to keep macular degeneration at bay. Beta-carotene is also included, which lowers the risk of cataracts.

Collard greens are a must-have for everyone who lives in Charleston, South Carolina. But the beauty of them is that they can sneak nutrition into even the most oblivious Southern palette.

Collards bind bile acids in the intestines and expel them in our stool, according to research. This lowers cholesterol while also lowering carcinogenic secondary bile acids.

Popeye obtained his superhuman power by popping a can of spinach, as you may recall. Popeye was first published in 1929, therefore this was quite innovative. And it is correct! One cup of cooked spinach has 36% of your daily iron need and 11% of your daily protein requirement, plus vitamins A and K, calcium, magnesium, potassium, and manganese. 4 grams of fiber, too.

Arugula is a cancer-fighting plant. It contains a unique combination of phytochemicals such as thiocyanates, sulforaphane, and indoles that may help fight malignancies such as prostate, breast, colon, ovarian, and cervical cancers. In a moment, we'll return to sulforaphane.

Bok choy: Bok choy is good for your bones since it contains important elements including iron, zinc, and magnesium, as well as vitamin K.

Grab some romaine if you want to have healthy skin and slow down the aging process. The vitamins A and C in romaine assist to lay down new collagen and neutralize oxidizing free radicals, preventing wrinkles. As a result, your skin will glow and be more supple.

Omega-3 Super Seeds (O)

This category is one of my favorites since I believe these foods have it all: they are healthful, delicious, varied, and unique. But first, a quick primer on omega-3 and omega-6 fatty acids. You've heard of trans, saturated, monounsaturated, and polyunsaturated fats. These omega-3 and -6 fats are polyunsaturated fats that are regarded "essential" since our bodies are unable to produce them on their own and must obtain them through our food. You can develop a deficiency if you don't consume them, which can lead to illness.

Polyunsaturated fats are generally considered healthful and are necessary for numerous bodily activities. However, omega-3s are perhaps more well-known than omega-6s. The modern Western diet delivers an excessive amount of omega-6s and an inadequate amount of omega-3s, which is why you've heard so much about omega-3s. The ratio of omega-6 to omega-3 fatty acids is a health indicator. Traditional societies are assumed to have evolved with a roughly equal mix of omega-6s and omega-3s, whereas most Westerners have a ratio of excess omega-6s of 15 to 16.7 to 1. It's a lopsided ratio that can lead to disease, such as cardiovascular disease, cancer, osteoporosis, and autoimmune diseases. Our goal is to achieve a balanced ratio, which necessitates an increase in omega-3s in our diet.

Omega-3 super seeds are exactly where we can locate them. To be particular, I'm talking about flaxseeds, chia seeds, and hemp seeds, which all include plant-based omega-3s. While both provide omega-3s, there are some distinctions between them, so let's take a closer look.

Flaxseed: Flaxseeds contain 2,300 milligrams of omega-3 alpha-linolenic acid (ALA) per tablespoon, making them a good source of ALA. It is, however, a good source of soluble fiber, which is one of the reasons it has been used as a traditional cure for constipation. Flax is also high in lignans, which are plant compounds that protect against hormone-related malignancies such as breast and prostate cancer.

Lignans can also be found in chia seeds, albeit the quantities are lower than in flax. Chia provides somewhat more omega-3s (2,400 mg per tablespoon vs. 2,300 mg per tablespoon) and much more fiber (5 grams in chia vs. 3 grams in flax). Chia seeds contain 40% fiber by weight, making them one of the world's best sources of fiber. This is primarily soluble fiber, a type of prebiotic fiber. If you stir a tablespoon of chia into a quarter cup of liquid and wait ten minutes, you'll see a viscous gel. Chia seeds have the ability to absorb ten to twelve times their own weight in water. Allow them to soak in water for a few hours to make chia pudding, which is healthful and similar to tapioca pudding in texture.

Last but not least, there are hemp seeds. They're not the same as flax and chia. Let me get this out of the way first. Hemp seeds, like marijuana, come from the same plant.

They are, nevertheless, legal! They are devoid of THC, the psychoactive component of cannabis. As a result, they will not make you high, but they will get you healthy. Hemp seeds provide roughly 40% of the omega-3 ALA found in chia and flax, although they are lower in fiber. Protein comes to mind when you think of hemp seeds. Hemp seeds are remarkable in that they are a complete protein, including all nine essential amino acids. As a result, hemp seeds provide both needed lipids and amino acids in one convenient package.

Aromatics (A) (Onions, Garlic)

These are the foods with flavor! Consider a rich, slow-simmered Italian sauce with plenty of garlic, onions, and basil.

Fresh herbs should always be used.

Herbs are loaded with nutrients. Basil contains anti-inflammatory, chemo preventive, radioprotective, antibacterial, analgesic, antipyretic, antidiabetic, hepatoprotective, hypolipidemic, and immunomodulatory characteristics due to its phytochemical content. Here's my point: whenever you get the chance to add fresh herbs and spices to a dish, take advantage of it! Flavor, plant diversity, and various phytochemicals are all added.

Because onions and garlic are both allium vegetables, they have a wonderful flavor. Leeks, shallots, chives, and scallions are other vegetables in this category that have similar health advantages. Allium veggies are high in vitamins B1, B2, B3, B6, C, E, and K, as well as folate, iron, magnesium, phosphorus, sodium, and zinc. Jam. Packed.

But then comes the truly wonderful stuff. Allium includes aromatic organosulfur compounds, which are responsible for its scent, flavor, and health benefits. An enzyme called alliinase is activated when fresh garlic or onions are diced or crushed, and it transforms alliin to allicin. Allicin, a molecule with antibacterial, antifungal, antiparasitic, and even antiviral effects, takes 10 minutes for the enzyme to activate. The more potent the odor, the better for your health. Before cooking with alliums, chop, then stop and wait ten minutes for allicin to activate. Multidrug-resistant enterotoxigenic E. coli and Candida albicans appear to be targets of allicin. It also encourages the growth of Bifidobacterial and other beneficial bacteria in the stomach. It's also worth noting that alliums are a good source of prebiotic fiber.

Garlic is my secret weapon when it comes to fighting the common cold.

We have a family tradition of utilizing garlic to treat common colds. We begin taking garlic at the first indication of a sore throat. Basically, two to four garlic cloves will be sliced into pill-size bits. After that, STOP. Allow ten minutes for the alliinase to activate the allicin before swallowing the capsule whole. I'll do this every day until the cold is gone, and I've successfully reversed colds by taking garlic pieces as soon as symptoms appear. My experience is backed up by a placebo-controlled trial. However, you do have a garlic-like odor while speaking. It's a small cost to pay.

Allium vegetables have anticancer properties, especially against stomach and prostate cancer. The anticancer action is divided into two levels. To begin, organosulfur compounds such as allicin detoxify carcinogens, inhibit tumor growth, and limit blood flow to tumors. Second, allium vegetables contain at least 24 flavonoid compounds, including quercetin. Anthocyanidins, which are found in red onions, are a bonus. Flavonoids have anti-inflammatory properties that may aid in cancer prevention.

These antioxidant chemicals appear to be helpful in the treatment of Alzheimer's disease and heart disease.

Onions (pro tip)

When you cut an onion, a process occurs that produces the organ sulfides that cause your eyes to weep. We appreciate these chemicals because they are cancer-fighting and anti-inflammatory. If you're having trouble cutting your onion, put it in the freezer for five minutes to cool it down before cutting. It's best to consume allium vegetables raw to receive the most benefits, but if that's not possible, cut them and let them sit to produce the compounds before cooking. (CHOP and STOP.)

Legumes (L)

Legumes are one of the world's healthiest foods. They're also dirt inexpensive! They include plenty of prebiotic fiber and resistant starches, which are essential for a healthy gut microbiome. Please don't miss out on the chance to strengthen your gut with these essential meals.

SULFORAPHANE (Sulforaphane) (Broccoli Sprouts and Other Cruciferous Veggies)

Plants remind me of my children. I adore them all, and I recognize the beauty in their differences. But if there's one I really like, it's this one. I've been waiting eight chapters to tell you about the amazing chemical sulforaphane found in cruciferous veggies.

Broccoli, kale, arugula, cabbage, cauliflower, and Brussels sprouts are all nutritious vegetables. But what makes them so unique? They're members of the cruciferous vegetable family. There are at least forty members of the family, yet they all have a common ancestor. Plants have evolved a common defensive strategy that uses an enzyme called myrosinase to transform glucosinolates into "toxic" chemicals during billions of years of evolution. Because myrosinase and glucosinolates are housed in separate compartments inside the plant, they don't interact under normal conditions. When an insect or invading herbivore—like yours truly—attacks the plant, the dividing chambers are broken, the chemicals are mixed, and a chemical reaction occurs, producing isothiocyanates (ITCs) like sulforaphane. It's similar to a bomb in terms of concept. So, what happens if the bomb detonates and these ITCs are released? Cancer is treated, inflammation is reduced, hearts are strengthened, blood sugar levels are reduced, fat is burned, and hormones are restored. ITCs are extremely beneficial to one's health. Another example of a plant's defense system simultaneously serving as our defense against cancer cells is this.

Let's talk about sulforaphane, my favorite isothiocyanate. cruciferous vegetables like broccoli, Brussels sprouts, kale, and cabbage contain sulforaphane. When Dr. Paul Talalay, a genuine pioneer in the field of cancer prevention, first published on the cancer-protective benefits of sulforaphane in

1992, he unlocked Pandora's box. Since then, hundreds of laboratory, animal, and human studies (many led by Dr. Talalay, who just died at the age of 95) have suggested that sulforaphane is the driving force behind these exceptionally beneficial foods. Here's what we've discovered about the therapeutic phytochemical sulforaphane:

Inhibits the production of carcinogens, activates enzymes to detoxify the carcinogens that are produced, shuts down blood flow to the tumor (which is needed to fuel growth), inhibits cancer cell migration and invasion, promotes cancer cell self-destruction (apoptosis), and even regulates cancer development through epigenetics to protect us from cancer.

Lung, colon, breast, prostate, skin, pancreas, liver, throat, and bladder cancers, as well as osteosarcoma, glioblastoma, leukemia, and melanoma—and maybe others—are all harmed.

Pro-inflammatory mechanisms that are triggered by bacterial endotoxin are shut off.

Detoxifies free radicals and reduces cellular damage as a potent antioxidant. Parkinson's disease, as well as stroke, concussion, and other brain injuries, may benefit.

In Alzheimer's patients, it reduces amyloid beta plaques and improves cognitive impairment. Improves anxiety and sadness, as well as mood. Improves memory and focus by enhancing brain function. Improves autoimmune illnesses including experimental multiple sclerosis and rheumatoid arthritis by regulating the immune system.

Reduces pathogenic harmful bacteria in the stomach and limits bacterial endotoxin release, among other methods, to put the body into fat-burning mode and encourage weight loss.

Inhibits the growth of germs and fungi. Twenty-three of the twenty-eight pathogenic bacterial and fungal species were suppressed in one investigation.

Improves lipids, lowers blood pressure, inhibits platelet aggregation, and even directly suppresses inflammation in the arteries to protect the heart.

Corrects type 2 diabetes by improving insulin sensitivity.

Diabetes damage is repaired, including diabetic heart and kidney damage. Protects the liver and kidneys against the side effects of certain chemotherapy medicines.

I could keep going, believe it or not. So, how does sulforaphane interact with the bacteria in our gut? Sulforaphane has been shown to reduce harmful bacteria numbers and bacterial endotoxin production. But there's a lot more to it. In another study, sulforaphane reversed leaky gut by upregulating tight junction formation and enhancing healthy gut bacteria, butyrate release, and intestinal lining repair to restore gut dysbiosis. Blown mind. What I'm saying is that sulforaphane works its utter magic in part by joining up with SCFAs to form the most potent gut-healing superhero combination ever.

Broccoli, Brussels sprouts, cabbage, cauliflower, and kale are all high in cruciferous vegetables. However, one meal stands out above the rest in terms of sulforaphane content: broccoli sprouts. These are immature broccoli, meaning the seed has only recently hatched and we are dealing with the earliest form of the plant. Bean sprouts and alfalfa sprouts are similar in idea. Sulforaphane levels in broccoli sprouts can be ten to one hundred times higher than in mature broccoli. This indicates that you can have the same benefit by eating large amounts of fully mature broccoli or a tiny number of broccoli sprouts.

Broccoli sprouts have a bitter, peppery flavor, but it's that bitterness that is destroying cancer cells for you. Also, taking a supplement instead of broccoli sprouts will not have the same impact. The genuine thing won out in a research comparing broccoli sprouts versus a supplement. Whole foods triumph once more! If the flavor of broccoli sprouts bothers you, consider incorporating them into a smoothie, soup, or larger salad.

Seaweed is deserving of more respect. It's a vegetable, not a weed. It just so happens to be a product of the sea. And, if we're talking about plant-based diversity, seaweed is a great way to get it because it not only has a lot of fiber, but it also contains three different types of fiber that you won't find in terrestrial plants—ulvans, xylans, and agars. These fibers are naturally prebiotic. Brown algae, such as kelp or wakame, have a unique component called fucoxanthin, which aids in fat reduction, weight loss, insulin sensitivity, and improved blood lipid profiles. Sea vegetables are also a good source of iodine and vitamin B12 for thyroid function.

You might be unsure where to begin with sea vegetables and algae because they aren't a common element of the American diet. Don't be concerned. Let's take a brief look at various options and how to use them.

Nori: These are the hard sheets that can be softened and used to form sushi rolls. They're a light, healthy snack on their own, but they may also be broken into "flakes" and sprinkled on salads for extra crunch.

Including F GOALS in your regular activities

So now that we have our list of core foods, it's time to change our eating habits. On the F GOALS list, pay attention to the fiber and FODMAP content.

It's no surprise that these meals are high in fiber and low in FODMAPs. FODMAPs aren't the enemy; they're our friends, as we've discussed. However, when it comes to fiber and FODMAPs, we want to start small and build up slowly.

FODMAPs Could Be Our Allies

You've probably heard about FODMAPs before, especially if you've ever sought treatment for digestive issues. Dairy (lactose) and gluten are the two most commonly mentioned foods when someone has a sensitive gut.

They're both classified as FODMAPs, and we'll talk about them and others shortly. Fermentable oligosaccharides, disaccharides, monosaccharides, and polyols are referred to as FODMAPs.

Simple sugars, sugar alcohols, or short chains of sugars (two to ten) that are connected together are what we're talking about. Because they behave similarly in the intestine, we've grouped them together.

Because FODMAPs are poorly absorbed, they draw water into the intestine. They can produce diarrhea in this manner. Our gut microorganisms can also ferment them, resulting in the generation of gas such as methane, carbon dioxide, and hydrogen. As a result of a combination of solids, liquids, and gases, FODMAPs can cause the gut to become inflated. Pain, bloating, and a pregnant-like tummy are all symptoms of distention (even in a guy). The extra water in our bowels promotes diarrhea, while methane gas slams on the motility brakes, causing constipation. Who will emerge victorious? Only time will tell, but one thing is certain: it's a sloppy mess inside.

It's no surprise that eliminating FODMAPs has been linked to a reduction in digestive problems. The low FODMAP diet, developed by a research team at Monash University in Melbourne, Australia, has been shown in randomized controlled trials to alleviate irritable bowel syndrome symptoms. Abdominal pain, bloating, and general symptoms all improve.

We're going to employ the GROWTH approach to Restrict, Observe, and Work It Back In rather than simply eliminating FODMAPs to end your awful digestive symptoms. Let me explain why.

There are five different FODMAPs. They are:

O-Oligosaccharides(Between three and 10 sugars are linked together.)

Fructans are fructose chains linked together that must be metabolized by intestinal bacteria. Garlic, onions, wheat, asparagus, and artichokes all contain fructans. FOS and inulin, both used as food additives, are fructans.

Galactans (or GOS) are galactose-chained carbohydrates that must be processed by gut bacteria. They're mostly found in legumes like peas, lentils, and beans.

D-Disaccharides (Two sugars are linked.)

Lactose is a sugar found in milk and other dairy products. Lactase, a digestive enzyme found in the small intestine, is required for absorption. Lactose that is not absorbed may be digested by the intestinal flora.

M-Monosaccarides a single sugar

Most fruits, some vegetables, and honey contain fructose.Mangoes are special in that they contain only fructose and no other FODMAPs. Fructose has also been artificially altered to create high-fructose corn syrup.

P-Polyols are sugar alcohols whose names usually end in "-ol."

BREAKFAST:

LOX OF CARROT

The ideal complement to toasted sourdough bread or piled-high bagels with your favorite toppings. The oil adds to the characteristic oily fish flavor, but you can leave it out if you want. A pinch of kelp powder added to the marinade will add a fishy flavor. For no-fishy sticks, use leftover kelp powder on baked tofu.

It serves 4 people.

4 big washed carrots

1/4 cup salt (coating)

3 tablespoons extra virgin olive oil

A quarter-teaspoon of lemon zest

1 tablespoon lemon juice, freshly squeezed

1/4 teaspoon paprika (smoked)

black pepper, freshly ground

1 tbsp. kelp powder (optional)

It's been boosted! (insert optional components here)

Onions, green and/or red

Onions pickled

Capers

Slices of jalapeo and/or tomato

Sprouts of onion

1. Preheat the oven to 400 degrees Fahrenheit.

2. Sprinkle the salt over the carrots on a piece of aluminum foil large enough to wrap them in. Fold the foil around the carrots and tuck the edges in to form a packet, then bake for 50 to 70 minutes, or until the carrots are easily punctured with a fork. Carrots that are larger will take longer to cook, but be careful not to overcook them to mush.

Alternatively, line the bottom of a small baking dish with parchment paper and sprinkle with salt. Sprinkle additional salt on top of the carrots. Cook exactly as suggested. This step can be completed a day in advance.

3. Whisk together the olive oil, lemon zest, lemon juice, paprika, pepper, and kelp powder, if using, while the carrots are boiling.

4. When the carrots are cool enough to handle, brush off the salt and pat them dry. The skin should have come off with the salt, but if it didn't, rub or peel it off gently. Slice the carrot into long strips as finely as possible using a sharp knife (or a sharp peeler).

5. Gently toss the carrot slices in the marinade until they are evenly covered. Allow for at least two hours of marinating time, or overnight in the refrigerator. The carrot lox will last a few days in the fridge and is best served at room temperature.

6. Spread a big schmear of avocado or plain dairy-free cream cheese on toasted bagels or sourdough bread. Make your supercharge options as unique as possible! Dill, capers, sliced jalapeos, and tomato slices are just a few of the options. Onions come in four varieties: green, red, pickled, and sprouting.

PLANT POINTS: 2

Super Seedy Porridge

Hemp and chia seeds are high in ALA, making this a wonderfully seedy breakfast porridge. While the ingredient list appears to be lengthy, it consists primarily of spices and flavorings. You can substitute pumpkin pie spice for the ginger, cinnamon, and nutmeg if you have any on hand.

Add maple syrup to taste if you prefer a sweeter porridge. Fresh berries and a sprinkle of nut butter on top are our favorite toppings.

It serves 2 people.

- A third cup of rolled oats
- 1/2 cup almond milk, unsweetened
- 2 teaspoons coarsely chopped raw pepitas
- 1 tsp. ginger powder
- 1 tsp cinnamon powder
- A pinch of nutmeg
- hemp seeds, 2 tablespoons
- 1 tablespoon almond butter + a little extra for serving
- chia seeds, 2 tablespoons
- 1/2 teaspoon extract de vanille
- 100% pure maple sugar (optional)
- Serve with berries

In a medium saucepan over medium high heat, bring the oats and 2/3 cup water to a boil. Reduce the heat to low and add the almond milk, pepitas, ginger, cinnamon, and nutmeg, stirring constantly. Cook for about 5 minutes, stirring occasionally, until the oats are soft.

Remove the pan from the heat and add the hemp seeds, almond butter, chia seeds, and vanilla extract. Taste and adjust the sweetness with maple syrup if desired.

If preferred, top with berries and more almond butter drizzling.

PLANT POINTS: 6

Coconut Cream Pudding with Pineapple

W e adore the tropical combination of pineapple and coconut, but 30 raspberries or a heaping 14 cup of blueberries are also Week 1–friendly topping options.

It serves 2 people

2 cups almond milk, unsweetened

chia seeds (1/4 cup)

2 teaspoons flaxseed powder

1 tablespoon maple syrup (100%) (optional)

1 teaspoon essence of vanilla

2 tablespoons unsweetened shredded coconut

2 cups pineapple slices

1 chopped date

Shake vigorously to incorporate the almond milk, chia seeds, flax meal, maple syrup, if using, and vanilla in a big mason jar with a cover. Remove from the fridge after 20 minutes and shake again. Return to the fridge for at least 30 minutes, or up to 24 hours.

Divide into two bowls, toss in the coconut, and top with pineapple and sliced dates when ready to serve.

Reduce the total amount of pineapple to 1 cup for **a low FODMAP option.**

Because dates are a high-FODMAP food, restrict your serving size to 13 chopped dates per meal in Week 1. Increase your serving size to 12 date in Week 2. If dates are not a trigger food, you can eat a complete date after Week 3.

Packing Tip: Make this in the evening in your favorite glass container with a lid, add the toppings in the morning, and pack it for busy mornings!

PLANT POINTS: 4

Smoothie with Superfoods

This smoothie is dubbed a "superfood" smoothie for a reason: it's jam-packed with all the good stuff: Hemp seeds, spinach, broccoli sprouts, berries, and satiating peanut butter are all high in ALA. Weeks 1 and 2 may require a touch of maple syrup if you prefer your smoothie to be sweeter. You can then add extra berries or kiwi and leave out the sweetener entirely.

It serves 1 people

1 quart of almond milk

hemp seeds, 2 tablespoons

1/2 cup leaves of spinach

Broccoli sprouts, small handful

5 medium strawberries 1 kiwi, skin removed

peanut butter, 2 teaspoons

1/2 bananas, frozen

A teaspoon to two tablespoons 100% pure maple sugar (optional)

In a blender, purée all of the ingredients until very smooth and creamy. You may need to add more liquid depending on the power of your blender. Reduce the liquid by half (use 1/2 cup almond milk) to make a smoothie bowl, then blend as indicated. Divide the mixture into two bowls, drizzle with peanut butter, and top with additional berries if desired. More fresh fruit, seeds, nut butter, and **Granola with Crispy Oats** can be added as garnish.

Packing Tip: Put the smoothie or bowl in a lidded mason jar or other leak-proof container. Pack toppings in a separate leak-proof container for the bowl, then combine when ready to eat.

FODMAP content of unripe bananas is lower than that of ripe bananas. Low FODMAP foods include half a ripe banana and one medium unripe banana. If you are fructose intolerant, use 1/2 bananas.

PLANT POINTS: 6

Sweet Potato Toast with Berries

While we prefer sourdough, this sweet potato variation of French toast is a great change of pace. We're serving it with almond butter and blueberries, but beyond Week 1, the topping options are unlimited. This recipe contains make-before instructions for parbaking sweet potatoes ahead of time and toasting them when ready to eat.

To cut the potatoes into slabs, you'll need a sharp knife, or a mandoline for more consistent slices.

Approximately 10 to 11 slices

- 1 big cleaned and dried sweet potato
- Almond butter, 2 teaspoons
- A dozen blueberries

Preheat the oven to 350 degrees Fahrenheit. Set a wire rack on top of a large rimmed baking sheet.

Trim the sweet potato's ends with a knife, then cut it lengthwise into 14-inch-thick slabs with a knife or mandoline.

Place the slabs in a single layer on the wire rack (or directly on the baking sheet) in the middle of the oven. Cook for 15 to 20 minutes, or until the potatoes are soft but not totally cooked, checking for burns every 5 minutes. Thinner potatoes will take less time to cook, whereas fatter potatoes will take longer. If you don't have a wire rack, flip the potatoes halfway through the cooking time.

Remove from the oven and cool completely on a wire rack before transferring to an airtight container and refrigerating for up to 4 days.

When ready to serve, toast the sweet potato slices (approximately 2 slices is a decent serving size) in a toaster or toaster oven on the medium setting until hot and crispy (cook time will vary depending on toaster). Serve with blueberries and almond butter.

Low FODMAP Option: Limit sweet potato portions to 1/2 cup for the first week (4 ounces). This will keep the sweet potato portion size modest in FODMAPs.

It's been boosted!

For more Plant Points and nutrients, top this toast with a dash of cinnamon, a sprinkle of unsweetened coconut flakes, or even a few hemp seeds.

PLANT POINTS: 3

TOAST WITH AVOCADO AND MUSHROOMS

It serves 2 people

This avocado toast is more of a fork-and-knife affair.'

Mushrooms, on the other hand, are fungus, not plants. However, they're high in prebiotic polysaccharides like - and -glucans, as well as chitin, which feed our gut microorganisms and aid in the creation of short-chain fatty acids. As a result, they're plainly deserving of +1 Plant Point.

1 tsp olive oil or 1 tblsp vegetable broth

8 ounces finely sliced button or baby bella mushrooms, stems removed

2 minced garlic cloves

2 large slices sourdough bread, or sourdough bread baked from scratch

1 avocado, large and ripe

1 teaspoon lemon juice, freshly squeezed

black pepper, freshly ground

1. HEAT THE OLIVE OIL in a large skillet over medium heat. Cook for 8 to 10 minutes, until the mushrooms begin to brown and the liquid has evaporated, adding a pinch of salt as needed. Cook for another minute or two, until the garlic cloves are warmed through.

2. Butter the sourdough bread and toast it. While the bread is browning, mash the avocado with a good amount of salt and pepper and spread it on the toast.

3. Toss in the heated mushrooms and top with supercharged garnishes.

PLANT POINTS: 5+

Granola with Crispy Oats

This granola is a fantastic addition to smoothies and smoothie bowls. We also enjoy this crisp, mildly sweet granola on its own or with a splash of plant-based milk. We love the acidic, sweet flavor and chewy texture of the cranberries, which are an optional addition.

$4^{1/4}$ cup yield

2 cups oats, rolled

1 cup shredded unsweetened coconut

1 cup walnuts, chopped

chia seeds, 2 teaspoons

hemp seeds, 2 tablespoons

2 teaspoons flaxseed powder

1 teaspoon cinnamon powder

3 tablespoons salt

2 tablespoons sunflower oil (organic)

1/4 cup maple syrup, 100 percent

1 teaspoon essence of vanilla

1/2 cup cranberries, dried (optional)

Preheat the oven to 250 degrees Fahrenheit. Using paper, line a rimmed baking sheet.

Combine the oats, coconut, walnuts, chia seeds, hemp seeds, flaxseed, cinnamon, and salt in a large mixing dish.

Whisk the sunflower oil and maple syrup together in a small saucepan over medium heat. Bring to a low boil, then remove from the heat and stir in the vanilla extract.

Mix the oat ingredients completely with the syrup mixture. On the prepared baking sheet, spread the granola in a single layer. Bake for 90 minutes, or until golden brown, stirring every 15 minutes.

Allow it cool completely before adding the dried cranberries (if using). Refrigerate for several weeks or freeze for up to three months after transferring to an airtight container.

Make-Ahead Suggestions: This dish makes a lot. We recommend cooking this at the beginning of Week 1 and eating it throughout the week. To keep it from drying out, keep it in an airtight container.

FODMAP-free Low FODMAP option: 1 tablespoon dried cranberries per serving.

PLANT POINTS: 6

TOAST OF HARISSA WHITE BEANS

*I*t serves 2 people

Red chili peppers are thought to be longevity foods. People who ingested red hot chili peppers had a 13 percent lower risk of death during the research, according to a large population-based prospective study with 273,877 person-years of follow-up.

1 tsp olive oil or 1 tsp broth

1 big minced garlic clove

$1^{1/4}$ cup drained and rinsed canned white beans or chickpeas

1–2 tablespoons harissa paste

1–2 tbsp. tahini or plain nondairy yogurt

1 lime's juice

A pinch of salt

2 slices sourdough bread, or sourdough bread baked from scratch

1. IN A MEDIUM SKILLET, heat the oil over medium heat. Cook for 30 seconds, stirring constantly, until the garlic is aromatic.

2. Stir in the beans and simmer for a few minutes, until they are warmed through and slightly crunchy around the edges. Combine the harissa paste, tahini, lime juice, and salt in a mixing bowl.

Reduce the heat to low and keep warm, adding extra harissa, lime, or tahini as needed for spice, tang, or creaminess.

3. Spread the warmed harissa beans on top of the toast. As desired, top with enhanced toppings.

PLANT POINTS: 5+

VEGETABLE CREPES WITH BUCKWHEAT

These are perfect for a savory weekend brunch or breakfast. You'll adore these crepes if you like conventional stuffed omelets. It's all plant-based food that doesn't attempt to be anything it isn't. Use a nonstick pan lightly coated with cooking spray or a very thin layer of olive oil to coat the pan for optimum results.

This recipe makes 2 or 3 crepes.

A third of a cup of all-purpose flour

buckwheat flour (3/4 cup)

1 teaspoon powdered baking soda

1 tablespoon flaxseed, ground

A quarter teaspoon of garlic powder

$1^{1/2}$ cup unsweetened almond milk (or other unsweetened nondairy milk of choice), plus additional as needed

A quarter teaspoon of salt

For sautéing, use olive oil or vegetable broth.

1 shallot 1 shallot

1/2 cup red bell pepper, chopped

1 cup button or baby bella mushrooms, sliced

1/2 cup zucchini, chopped

salt and black pepper, freshly ground

Grease the skillet with cooking spray or olive oil.

A quarter cup of cashew cream

Garnish with fresh flat-leaf parsley, microgreens, and/or sprouts

1. In a large mixing bowl, whisk together the flours, baking powder, flaxseed, garlic powder, almond milk, and salt until smooth. The consistency should be similar to pancake batter. If the sauce is too thick, add extra milk.

2. Coat a big skillet with a thin layer of olive oil and heat over medium heat. Cook for 10 minutes, until the shallot, bell pepper, mushrooms, and zucchini are tender, with a pinch of salt and pepper. Season to taste, and season with extra salt or pepper if necessary. Remove from the equation.

3. Lightly coat a big nonstick skillet with cooking spray or a very thin layer of olive oil and heat it over medium heat.

4. Pour in a third to half of the crepe batter (depending on the size of your pan) and tilt the skillet to distribute the batter as much as possible to the sides. Cook for 3 minutes on the bottom, then turn and cook for another 2 to 3 minutes until set. Continue with the remaining batter.

5. To serve, spread a dollop of cashew cream over the crepes and top with the cooked vegetable combination, fresh parsley, microgreens, and/or sprouts.

PRO TIP: Blend 14 cup raw cashews, 14 cup water, 12 tablespoon freshly squeezed lemon juice, 14 teaspoon chopped garlic, and a pinch of salt until very creamy and smooth to make cashew cream. Dairy-free cream cheese can be used as a quick substitution.

PLANT POINTS: 5+

Bowls of Tofu Scramble

This is going to be your new favorite brunch. When compared to eggs, tofu is lower in saturated fat, lower in monounsaturated fat, higher in polyunsaturated fats, and cholesterol-free, making it the ideal substitute.

If this is your first time cooking with tofu, be aware that you will need to press it first. You can use a tofu press or wrap the tofu block in paper towels, place it on a rimmed baking sheet, and top it with something heavy. Allow 10 minutes for the majority of the water to drain. This makes the tofu more chewy, which is ideal for egg-like curds.

It serves 2 people

veggie broth, 5 teaspoons

8 oz. firm tofu, crumbled or diced after draining, pressing, and crumbling

1 scallion, chopped only the green portions

1/2 teaspoon paprika (smoked)

1/2 teaspoon turmeric powder

1/4 teaspoon cumin powder

salt and black pepper, freshly ground

2 cubed leftover pieces of **Sweet Potato Toast with Berries**

2 cups kale, coarsely chopped (stems removed)

Heat 2 tablespoons vegetable broth in a medium skillet over medium heat until it shimmers. Cook for 2 minutes until the tofu is warmed, then add the scallions, paprika, turmeric, cumin, and a touch of salt. Reduce the heat to low and simmer for another 5 minutes, stirring regularly.

Heat the remaining 3 tablespoons broth in a separate skillet over medium heat.

Cook, stirring occasionally, until the sweet potatoes are heated, about 5 minutes. Cover with the greens and a touch of salt and pepper. Cook for 3 minutes, or until the greens have wilted slightly.

In two bowls, divide the kale and sweet potatoes, then top with the tofu mixture. Add a slice of sourdough toast, with or without peanut or almond butter, for a heartier supper.

It's been boosted!

Add chopped parsley, cilantro, and diced tomatoes to the top.

PLANT POINTS: 3

TOAST WITH AVOCADO IN THE SUMMER

It serves 2 people

These lovely summer tomato slices atop a perfectly ripe avocado, topped with a few garnishes.

2 slices sourdough bread, or sourdough bread baked

1/2 avocados, huge and ripe

4 good-quality tomato slices

vinegar balsamic

1 tsp flaky salt

black pepper, freshly cracked

It's been boosted! (optional garnishes):

Sprouts

Garlic, minced

Extra-virgin olive oil is a type of extra-virgin olive oil that is

basil leaves

Arugula

Sauerkraut

The avocado should be spread on top of the toast after it has been toasted. Drizzle a little balsamic vinegar over the tomatoes, along with a liberal sprinkling of flaky salt and crushed black pepper. Optional toppings can be added at any time.

PLANT POINTS: 3+

SOURDOUGH BREAD MADE WITH WHOLE WHEAT

A sourdough made entirely of whole wheat flour is extremely tough. This recipe calls for both regular bread flour and whole-wheat flour. Bread flour contains more gluten than all-purpose flour and should not be substituted with another flour for optimal results.

Active sourdough starter, 50 grams (1/4 cup)

350 g ($1^{1/2}$ cup) warm water (about 85°F)

Bread flour, 400 grams ($2^{1/2}$ cups)

Whole-wheat flour, 100 g (3/4 cup)

Fine sea salt, 7 grams ($1^{1/4}$ tablespoons)

1. IN A LARGE MIXING basin, combine the sourdough starter and water.

2. Add the flours and knead and squeeze the dough in circular motions with your hands until no dry lumps remain. Cover and set aside for 20 minutes to allow the flour to absorb all of the liquid before proving. Sprinkle the salt evenly across the surface and whisk thoroughly to incorporate. Check on your dough at this moment. It should be shaggy; if it's tough to combine and work with inside the bowl, add more water in 20-gram (4-teaspoon) increments, thoroughly mixing until the dough is pliable and slightly sticky. When using whole-grain flour, you may need to use additional water to attain this consistency.

3. Cover with a damp cloth and set aside in a warm area for 1 hour.

4. Start with the stretches and folds. Wet your hands so they don't cling together, then take a bit of the dough from the bowl and stretch it upward and away from you, then fold it into the bowl's center.

Stretch and fold the dough toward the center, then turn the bowl a quarter turn and repeat. Turn the bowl a quarter turn and repeat, then do it again, for a total of four stretches and folds around the bowl.

5. Allow the dough to rest for 30 minutes before repeating the stretches and folds. Repeat the stretch-and-fold process two more times for a total of four sessions.

6. Cover the bowl and let it bulk rise in a warm place for 2 to 3 hours after your last series of stretches and folds. When it has grown by at least a third of its original size, it is ready. Cover the dough and set it in the refrigerator overnight to bake the next morning.

7. Remove the dough from the fridge in the morning and set it on a lightly floured surface. Allow 30 minutes to allow some of the chill from the fridge to go before shaping into a loose ball: Stretch and fold the dough toward the center, starting at the top. As you would when folding an envelope, start with the bottom of the dough, then the left side, and finally the right.

8. Scoop the dough with a bench knife or a flat spatula and flip it over so the smooth side is facing up. Cover and set aside for 30 minutes more.

9. Prepare a flour-dusted banneton proofing basket. Alternatively, dust a medium bowl with flour after lining it with cotton or linen cloth.

Remove from the equation. Using the same envelope approach as before, re-shape the dough. Turn it over, then gently cup the dough in your hands and pull it in a circle form toward you. This will aid in the creation of dough tension and the creation of a circular form. Scoop the dough into the prepared bowl with the smooth side facing up, using the bench knife or spatula from previously. Cover and set aside for another 30 to 1 hour. When you gently poke the dough with your finger, it should look puffy and feel like an inflated water balloon.

10. Preheat the oven to 450°F near the end of the last rise. Cut a sheet of parchment paper to fit a Dutch oven or other baking vessel ,leaving enough space around the sides to remove the bread easily.

11. Invert the bowl and place the parchment paper over the dough to release it.

Dust the dough with flour and work it into the bread gently with your hands. Make a few shallow slashes in the dough with a bread lame, razor, or extremely sharp paring knife to allow for expansion. Here you are free to be as inventive as you wish. Make four shallow cuts at 12 o'clock, 3 o'clock, 6 o'clock, and 9 o'clock for convenience. To transfer the dough to the baking pot, use the parchment paper overhang.

12. Cover with a tight-fitting lid and set on a baking pan, then bake for 20 minutes at 350°F. Remove the lid and bake for another 40 minutes, or until the top is golden brown.

13. Take out of the oven and set aside to cool for at least an hour. Before slicing the bread, it needs to rest.

PLANT POINTS: 1

LUNCH

Salad for Every Day :

W e call this the daily salad because we feel that eating fresh veggies every day is beneficial, and what better way to do so than with a Fiber Fueled salad? This is the dish to make if you want something hearty, satisfying, and quick to make. This recipe calls for pickled beets. Even though simple beets are rich in FODMAP, they are low in them.

It serves 2 people

Salad

4 cups leafy greens, chopped

1/2 cup pickled beets (recipe below) or store-bought

1/2 cup chickpeas, cooked

sunflower seeds, 1/4 cup

Broccoli sprouts, a handful

1 shredded medium carrot

10 sliced cherry tomatoes

Orange Dressing without Oil

1/4 cup orange juice, freshly squeezed

apple cider vinegar, 2 tablespoons

tahini (2 tablespoons)

1/4 teaspoon salt, plus additional salt to taste

1/4 teaspoon black pepper, freshly ground, plus more to taste

For serving, Energized Roasted Roots (recipe follows).

Toss the greens, pickled beets, chickpeas, sunflower seeds, sprouts, carrots, tomatoes, and any additional Supercharge toppings, if using, in a large mixing dish. Place aside.

Make the dressing as follows: In a small dish or mason jar, whisk together the orange juice, vinegar, tahini, salt, and pepper until smooth. Whisk in 1 spoonful of water at a time until you get the desired consistency (the dressing should be pourable but not runny). Season with salt and pepper to taste. The dressing will keep in the fridge for up to 5 days if used later.

When ready to serve, sprinkle 14 cup dressing over each salad, toss thoroughly, and season with salt and pepper to suit.

It's been boosted!

1 cup **Energized Roasted Roots,** parsley, and cubed, baked potatoes

tofu. After Week 2, you can add 12 avocado slices on top.

PLANT POINTS: 9

Beets Pickled Quickly

2 cups sliced steamed beets

1/4 cup red wine vinegar plus 2 teaspoons

1 tablespoon maple syrup (100%)

1 tablespoon spice for pickling (see Note)

In a small saucepan, bring the cooked beets, vinegar, maple syrup, and pickling spice to a boil over high heat. Reduce the heat to low and cook for 3 minutes, covered. Allow to cool for 30 minutes after removing from the heat.

Beets can be kept in the fridge for up to a week.

Note: If you don't have pickling spice, a pinch of mustard seeds, two or three whole cloves, and a pinch of whole peppercorns would suffice.

Energized Roasted Roots

This topping is designed to improve the fiber content of your meals wherever you need it. Toss a handful into salads, **Bowls of Tofu Scramble** or eat them alone.

The approach can be applied on virtually any vegetable, though cooking times may need to be changed. This blend is excellent for Week 1, but the technique can be used on almost any vegetable out there.

It serves 4 people

2 cups sweet potato cubes

2 chopped parsnips

6 big sliced radishes

1 tablespoon extra virgin olive oil (or **garlic-infused extra virgin olive oil**)

2 tablespoons broth de légumes

Half teaspoon of salt

1/2 teaspoon pepper, freshly ground

Preheat the oven to 425 degrees Fahrenheit.

In a large mixing basin, add the sweet potato, parsnips, radishes, olive oil, broth, salt, and pepper. Place in a single layer on a rimmed baking sheet (you may need two, depending on size) and cover with foil.

Roast for 35 minutes, or until the vegetables are mostly tender. Remove the pan from the oven, remove the foil, and give it a good toss. Return the pan to the oven for another 10 minutes, or until the sides are lightly crisped.

PLANT POINTS: 3

Super Soup from the Wild Biome

This substantial soup is made with wild rice and chickpeas and is tasty and filling. While you can have this soup at any time of year, it's especially comforting on a chilly, rainy day.

It serves 2 people.

1 teaspoon extra virgin olive oil

2 sliced carrots

1 sliced celery stalk

2 teaspoons chopped fresh chives

1/4 teaspoon salt, plus additional salt to taste

1/8 teaspoon black pepper, freshly ground, plus more to taste

Broth from a Biome$(2^{1/2}$ cup$)$

a third of a cup of wild rice

chickpeas, 1/2 cup

1 cup kale, roughly chopped (stems removed)

Heat the olive oil in a medium saucepan over medium-high heat. Combine the carrots, celery, chives, salt, and pepper in a large mixing bowl. Cook until the vegetables are crisp-tender, 3 to 5 minutes.

Add the broth, rice, and 1/2 cup water to the pot. Bring the mixture to a boil, then reduce to a low heat setting and cover. Cook, stirring occasionally, for about 40 minutes, or until the rice has softened.

Cook, stirring occasionally, until the chickpeas and kale are barely wilted, about 5 minutes. Season to taste with salt and pepper.

Pack in a thermos to keep warm at work, or place in a leak-proof container and reheat just before serving. Bklyn Bento jars, which come with a bamboo spoon, and Lillie Home stainless-steel thermoses are two of our favorites.

It's been boosted!

Serve alongside a portion of sourdough bread and the **Dip in Muhammara** from the meal plan. Garnish with scallions that have been finely cut.

PLANT POINTS: 7

INDIAN CURRY WITH LOTS OF VEGETABLES

Although there are various variations of garam masala, the base is usually a combination of cumin, turmeric, chile, ginger, and garlic. If you don't have all of the spices, I've suggested substitutions.

It serves 4 people.

3 tblsp extra-virgin olive oil or 3 tblsp vegetable broth

3 cups cauliflower florets (about half of a large cauliflower head)

3 medium diced Yukon gold potatoes

3 medium carrots, peeled and sliced

1 medium sliced onion

1 teaspoon seeds of cumin

2 minced garlic cloves

1 tablespoon freshly grated ginger

1 teaspoon turmeric powder

1/4 teaspoon cayenne pepper (optional) or salt and pepper to taste

1/2 tbsp garam masala (or more curry powder, to taste)

1 teaspoon curry powder (yellow)

1/2 teaspoon coriander powder (optional)

1/2 teaspoon salt, plus additional salt to taste

1/4 teaspoon black pepper, freshly ground, plus more to taste

1 cup green peas, frozen

1 quart vegetable stock

1 cup coconut milk (optional) or more broth

1/2 tbsp lemon zest

1 tablespoon lemon juice, freshly squeezed

2 cups brown rice (cooked) for serving

For serving, fresh cilantro, chopped

1. Heat 2 teaspoons of olive oil in a large skillet over medium heat. Combine the cauliflower, potatoes, carrots, and onion in a large mixing bowl.

2. Cook, stirring occasionally, for about 7 minutes, or until the veggies start to brown. If the mixture begins to stick, a dash of vegetable broth can be added to loosen it up.

3. Push the mixture to the side of the pan, then add the cumin seeds and the remaining teaspoon of olive oil. Allow to crackle for about a minute, until fragrant, then incorporate into the vegetable mixture and heat for another minute, taking care not to burn the mixture.

4. Add the turmeric, cayenne, garam masala, yellow curry powder, coriander, salt, and pepper to taste. Cook for a further 5 to 10 minutes, stirring frequently, until the veggies are tender-crisp.

5. Stir in the coconut milk and cook for a few minutes more, until it has warmed up. Taste and season with more salt and pepper as needed after adding the lemon zest and juice.

6. Toss with chopped cilantro and serve over hot brown rice.

PLANT POINTS: 10

SALAD WITH LEMON AND LENTILS

The sweet potatoes and carrots feel like fall and winter vegetables, but the zucchini, yellow squash, and lemon are all summer staples.

It serves 4 people.

Note on FODMAPs: 1 cup diced zucchini is a low-FODMAP serving.

2 cups sweet potatoes, diced

2 medium diced carrots

1 small sliced zucchini

1 diced tiny yellow squash

1/4 teaspoon paprika (smoked)

1/2 teaspoon cumin powder

1/4 teaspoon salt plus additional salt for the dressing

1/4 teaspoon black pepper, plus more for the dressing

Olive oil is a type of oil that comes from (optional)

1 teaspoon mustard (Dijon)

2 tbsp tahini

2 tbsp lemon juice, freshly squeezed

1/4 cup fresh flat-leaf parsley, finely chopped

$1^{1/2}$ cup washed and drained canned lentils

1. PREHEAT THE OVEN to 400 degrees Fahrenheit. In a large mixing basin, combine the sweet potatoes, carrots, zucchini, and squash, along with the paprika, cumin, salt, and pepper.

Drizzle in the olive oil, if using, and toss well to evenly coat the spices. Bake for 25 to 30 minutes, until golden brown and soft, in a single layer on a large baking sheet.

2. Whisk together the mustard, lemon juice, tahini, and 2 tablespoons water until creamy and smooth while the veggies are cooking. Toss in the parsley and season to taste with salt and pepper.

3. Toss the canned lentils with the cooked veggies and serve with the dressing.

PRO HINT: Want to roast your vegetables without using any oil? Let's get started! Steam the starchy veggies (sweet potatoes and carrots) until they are just soft. In a large mixing bowl, combine them with your raw non-starchy vegetables (zucchini and squash) and enough moisture to allow the spices adhere. Toss in the spices from Step 1 and put aside for 10 to 20 minutes before roasting to allow the spices to absorb moisture. Boom! Delish.

UNLEASHED FF:

If you're not following a low-FODMAP diet, add additional zucchini and 1 garlic clove minced to the dressing.

PLANT POINTS: 8

SALAD WITH GREEK GRAINS

S ay that five times quickly! A Greek salad's taste combination is hard to beat—olives, cucumbers, basil, parsley, and a dash of lemon. It's important to note that the feta must be made at least an hour ahead of time, but it's well worth it. Reality can wait. Forget about the kids jumping on the couch with permanent markers.

It serves 4 people.

FODMAP note: A serving of 1/4 cup chickpeas is low in FODMAPs.

2 cups quinoa (cooked)

1/4 cup hemp seeds, hulled

1 cup cucumbers, diced

1/2 cup pitted black or Kalamata olives, sliced

1/2 cup green scallion tops, thinly sliced

1 chopped medium red bell pepper

1/2 cup fresh basil, freshly chopped

1/2 cup fresh flat-leaf parsley, freshly chopped

2 tbsp lemon juice, freshly squeezed

salt and black pepper, freshly ground

Extra-virgin olive oil is a type of extra-virgin olive oil that is (optional)

1/4 cup chickpeas, canned (optional)

Tofu Feta Made at Home (optional)

1. Combine the quinoa, hemp seeds, cucumbers, olives, scallions, bell pepper, basil, and parsley in a large mixing dish. Add the lemon juice and mix one more, then season with salt & pepper to taste. Drizzle with olive oil and mix once more if desired.

2. Serve with canned chickpeas or Homemade Tofu Feta, if desired.

FF UNLEASHED: If you're not following a low-FODMAP diet, you can increase the chickpeas and add diced tomato.

PLANT POINTS: 9+

Tofu Feta Made at Home

Before you start making this recipe, decide who you're going to call first to tell them you just enjoyed the most incredible plant-based feta. Let them know that sharing the Fiber Fueled tofu feta dish is an act of love. Yes, there are more!

1 tablespoon miso (white)

2 tbsp lemon juice, freshly squeezed

1 tablespoon vinegar (apple cider)

A Half-cup of nutritional yeast

1/2 teaspoon oregano, dry

A Half teaspoon of salt

1/4 teaspoon black pepper, freshly ground

Drained and pressed 8 ounces extra-firm tofu (see Pro Tip)

1. Whisk together the miso, 2 tablespoons water, lemon juice, vinegar, nutritional yeast, oregano, salt, and pepper in a mixing bowl until the miso is completely dissolved.

Crumble in the tofu, then slowly fold in the wet ingredients until the tofu is well covered.

2. Refrigerate for at least 1 hour after covering. As the feta rests, it becomes tastier!

PRO TIP: Pressing tofu removes extra moisture, making it firmer and better able to keep its shape. Tofu can be pressed or simply placed on a layer of paper towels, then covered with another layer of paper towels. Place something heavy on top, such as a large, thick book or some pantry cans. Allow at least 30 minutes for the paper towels to absorb any remaining moisture.

After that, cut the tofu into whichever shape you like and keep it in the fridge or freezer.

Sandwich with Muhammara

To make this sandwich for lunch, separate the toast, roasted Italian vegetables, spinach, and dip, then assemble just before eating. This is great as an open-faced sandwich.

It makes one sandwich.

Dip in Muhammara leftovers

Medley of Italian Roasted Vegetables Leftovers

Bread made with sourdough starter

Leaves of fresh spinach

Toast the bread and warm the dip and vegetables just before serving. On two pieces of bread, spread the muhammara dip, then arrange the vegetables and spinach leaves on top. Assemble, slice, and serve like an open-faced sandwich.

PLANT POINTS: 7

Kale Salad with a Twist

This is one of our favorite kale recipes! The avocado–almond butter dressing is rich, creamy, and flavorful. It's easy to make, full of flavor and texture, and packed with plant-based nutrients! Throughout the four-week plan, we utilize this as a side dish for numerous meals.

It serves 2 people

1 cup kale, rough stems removed and diced (dinosaur kale is excellent)

3 teaspoons tamari (low sodium)

1 cup spinach, chopped

chives (about 2 tblsp.)

a quarter teaspoon of salt

1/8 teaspoon black pepper, freshly ground

1/4 mashed avocado

almond butter, 2 tbsp

1/2 celery stalks, chopped

2 tbsp. walnuts, coarsely chopped (optional)

1/4 cup scallions, chopped (just green portions) (optional)

Drizzle 1 teaspoon tamari over the kale in a medium bowl and massage with your hands to soften and break down the greens. Toss in the spinach, chives, salt, and pepper one more time.

To thin, mash the avocado with the almond butter in a separate small bowl and whisk in the remaining 2 teaspoons of tamari.

Pour the avocado mixture over the kale and massage it in with your hands or tongs to fully coat each piece.

Serve with celery, walnuts, and scallions.

Alternative FODMAP Suggestions: If you can tolerate a larger piece of kale than 12 cup, do so, as this recipe creates a lot of dressing!

Make-Ahead Suggestions: This salad is fine for a day after it's made, but not for much longer. If you only want to eat half of the greens now and the other half later, dress half of the greens with half of the dressing and toppings. Separately store the leftover kale, spinach, dressing, chopped celery, walnuts, and scallions until ready to serve.

PLANT POINTS: 5

SALAD WITH HERBED POTATOES

A excellent herbed potato salad is hard to top as a complement to other summertime foods and is incredibly flexible.

1$^{1/2}$ pound scrubbed tiny red potatoes

Salt

1/3 cup flat-leaf fresh parsley, plus more to taste

1/4 cup scallions (white and green sections) thinly cut, plus more to taste

2 tablespoons lemon juice (plus more to taste)

1$^{1/2}$ tablespoons Dijon mustard, plus salt and pepper to taste

1 sliced garlic clove

black pepper, freshly ground, plus more to taste

A quarter cup of olive oil or a cup of broth

IT'S BEEN BOOSTED! (optional garnishes):

Tomatoes, cut in half

More scallions, sliced (white and green parts)

More herbs, chopped

1. Place the potatoes, a big amount of salt, and 2 inches of water in a large stock pot. Bring to a boil, then reduce to a low heat and cook, stirring occasionally, until the potatoes are barely soft, about 5 to 8 minutes.

2. Drain the potatoes, reserving 2 tablespoons of the boiling water, then cool and slice them into 14-inch slices.

3. In the base of a food processor, pulse the parsley, scallions, lemon juice, mustard, garlic, another teaspoon of salt, and a pinch of pepper 7 or 8 times until roughly chopped. Drizzle in the saved cooking water and olive oil while the machine is running to form a creamy sauce, stopping to scrape down the sides as needed.

4. Season with salt, lemon juice, mustard, parsley, or scallions to taste. Pour the sauce over the potatoes and mix in gently, being careful not to smash them. It's best served cold or at room temperature.

PRO TIP: This is a typical potato salad with parsley, but cilantro or basil can be substituted for a fresh touch.

DINNER

Plant-Powered Ragu de Polenta

Especially when coupled with our fast ragu of Italian veggies and lentils, creamy polenta is a stick-to-your-ribs comfort dish. Try this ragu with **Parmesan Pepitas** after one Week, a nutty parm that's great on everything from pasta to polenta to popcorn.

It serves 2 people

Ragu in a hurry

2 teaspoons extra virgin olive oil, **garlic-infused extra virgin olive oil,** or vegetable broth

1 cup tomatoes, chopped

salt and black pepper, freshly ground

1 cup lentils in a can

2 cups **Medley of Italian Roasted Vegetables**

1/2 teaspoon oregano powder, plus more to taste

1/2 teaspoon dried basil (more to taste)

red pepper flakes, crushed (optional)

Polenta

$1^{1/2}$ cup almond milk, unsweetened

A Half cup of cornmeal

A Half teaspoon of salt

black pepper, freshly ground

Parsley, chopped for dish

For serving, fresh basil, chopped

To make the ragu, combine all of the ingredients in a large mixing bowl. Add the olive oil to a medium saucepan and heat over medium heat. Add the tomatoes, a bit of salt, and a grind of black pepper. Cook for about 10 minutes, stirring frequently, until the tomatoes have broken down. In a large mixing bowl, combine the lentils, Roasted Italian Medley, oregano, basil, and red pepper flakes, if using. Cook for 10 minutes, or until thickened, stirring periodically. Taste as you go, and season with additional salt, pepper, and dry herbs as needed.

In a medium saucepan over medium heat, whisk together 12 cup water and the almond milk to make the polenta. Whisk in the cornmeal and salt when bubbles begin to appear. Reduce to a low heat and cook for 10 to 15 minutes, or until the sauce has thickened. Taste as you go, and season with extra salt and pepper if necessary.

Divide the polenta between two bowls and top with the ragu to serve. Garnish with parsley and basil, chopped fresh.

PLANT POINTS: 8

Taco Salad and Tempeh Tacos

The tempeh taco filling and creamy cilantro sauce are made to work in both tacos and taco salads. Make the entire recipe and portion half to save for later in the week to save time.

It serves 4 people

Filling for Tempeh Tacos

1 tablespoon extra virgin olive oil

8 oz. coarsely chopped tempeh

1 tablespoon cayenne pepper

2 tsp. paprika (smoked)

A Half teaspoon of salt

1/4 teaspoon cayenne pepper, ground

1 cup drained canned lentils

CILANTRO CREAM SAUCE

1 jalapeo, cut roughly

1/2 c. cilantro

slivered almonds (1/4 cup)

1 lime, zest and juice

1 teaspoon kosher salt

When it comes to tacos,

4 tortillas de maz

Serving salad with shredded lettuce, black olives, chopped tomatoes, scallions, and cilantro

Salad Dressing

4 cups lettuce, shredded

1/2 CUP TOMATOES, CRUMBLED

1/3 cup black olives, sliced

2 scallions, sliced (green parts only)

1/3 cup cilantro, chopped

Make the taco filling: In a large skillet over medium heat, heat the oil. Toss in the tempeh. Break it up with a wooden spoon, then mix in the chili powder, smoked paprika, salt, and cayenne pepper. Cook for 10 minutes, or until the tempeh is softened, adding a splash of broth or water if it adheres to the pan or becomes too dry. Stir in the lentils to mix and warm them through.

To make the creamy cilantro sauce, purée the jalapeos, cilantro, almonds, lime zest, lime juice, 1/2 cup water, and salt in a blender until smooth and creamy. It should have the consistency of a thick salad dressing. If the dressing is too thick, add 1 tablespoon of water at a time.

Warm the tortillas just before serving to assemble the tacos. Top the corn tortillas with half of the tempeh filling, shredded lettuce, tomatoes, olives, scallions, cilantro, and dressing. Half of the filling can be saved for taco salad later in the week.

Assemble the taco salad as follows: Combine the lettuce, tomatoes, olives, scallions, and cilantro in a mixing dish and divide into two bowls. Drizzle the cilantro dressing on top of the remaining tempeh taco filling.

Make-Ahead Suggestion:

Prepare the tempeh taco filling and creamy cilantro sauce up to 3 days ahead of time. Half of the tempeh taco filling and creamy cilantro dressing can be saved for Tempeh Taco Salad later in the week.

Chili powder may contain garlic, so examine the ingredient list and pay attention to how you feel after this meal if you're on a **low FODMAP diet**.

PLANT POINTS: 5+

Tomato Noodle Soup is a nourishing soup made with tomatoes.

This soul needs tomato noodle soup. This low-FODMAP soup is warming, nourishing, and downright tasty.

It serves 2 people

3 cups **Broth from a Biome**(plus more as necessary)

1 scallion, cut (just the green portion)

2 teaspoons ginger (freshly grated)

1 thinly diced Roma tomato

1 tblsp. soy sauce

6 ounces drained, lightly pressed (see Note), and finely sliced firm tofu

1/2 teaspoon turmeric powder

rice noodles, 5 oz.

miso paste, 2 tblsp.

1 teaspoon sesame oil, roasted (optional)

Energized Roasted Roots(optional) for serving

In a medium saucepan, heat 2 tablespoons of the broth over medium heat. Cook for about 10 minutes, until the tomato is well broken down, before adding the scallion leaves, ginger, tomato, and tamari. As needed, add a dash or two of broth.

Cook for another 1 to 2 minutes, stirring occasionally to avoid sticking. Bring the remaining stock, along with the turmeric, to a low boil. Allow about 10 minutes of simmering time for the flavors to meld.

Reduce to a low heat and stir in the rice noodles. Cook for a further 2 to 3 minutes, or until the noodles are soft and fully cooked.

Remove the pan from the heat and mix in the miso. If preferred, drizzle with sesame oil and top with the roasted roots to serve.

It's been boosted!

1 toasted nori slice, split into strips, sesame seeds, and sliced scallion greens on top

Slice tofu into slabs, then wrap in clean kitchen towels or paper towels to press. Cover with a heavy object, such as food cans or a pan, on a rimmed baking sheet. Allow to sit for 10 minutes, or until the majority of the water has evaporated.

PLANT POINTS: 5

Pasta with Pesto

U sing leftover **Medley of Italian Roasted Vegetables** from earlier in the week, this hearty pasta dish pulls together quickly.

It serves 4 people

Pesto with arugula and walnuts

3 cups arugula, packed

1/2 cup walnuts, gently roasted

a teaspoon of nutritious yeast

2 tbsp lemon juice, freshly squeezed

1/4 cup water or vegetable broth

1/4 teaspoon salt, plus additional salt to taste

1/4 teaspoon black pepper, freshly ground, plus more to taste

1 tablespoon extra virgin olive oil (optional)

8 oz. gluten-free pasta, dry

2 cups Italian Medley (Roasted) (recipe follows)

To make the pesto, pulse the arugula, walnuts, and nutritional yeast in a food processor until very finely chopped. Add the lemon juice, vegetable broth, salt, and pepper while the motor is running. To taste, season with extra salt and pepper. If using, drizzle with the olive oil and put aside.

A big saucepan of salted water should be brought to a boil. Cook until the pasta is just al dente, as directed on the package. Drain the noodles and save 12 cup of the pasta water.

Return the spaghetti to the pot and stir in the pesto. Toss with a few sprays of pasta water as needed to keep the spaghetti from sticking together. Serve with the remaining Roasted Italian Medley. Serve with crushed red pepper flakes if you want your pasta a little hot.

OPTIONS FOR LOW FODMAP Diets:

Quinoa pasta is available from both Ancient Harvest and NOW Foods. Chickpea spaghetti is also tasty, but with more than a 1-cup serving, it has a moderate FODMAP count.

PLANT POINTS: 6

Medley of Italian Roasted Vegetables

W eek 1 dinner prep will be made much easier with this one-pan side dish. These vegetables will appear in a variety of dishes, including the **Plant-Powered Ragu de Polenta**, the **Sandwich with Muhammara**, and the **<u>Pasta with Pesto.</u>**

6 cup yield

1 big cubed eggplant

2 medium diced zucchini

1 seeded and diced red bell pepper

2 diced Roma tomatoes

1 small fennel bulb, fronds trimmed and sliced ($1^{1/2}$ cup)

1 teaspoon Italian seasoning (dry)

1/4 CUP VEGAN BROTH

2 to 3 teaspoons extra virgin olive oil

A Half teaspoon of salt

1/2 teaspoon black pepper, freshly ground

1/4 teaspoon red pepper flakes, crushed (optional)

Preheat the oven to 400 degrees Fahrenheit.

Toss the eggplant, zucchini, bell pepper, Roma tomatoes, fennel, Italian seasoning, vegetable broth, olive oil, salt, black pepper, and red pepper flakes (if using) together in a large mixing bowl. Place on a rimmed baking sheet in a single layer (you may need two baking sheets, depending on the size), then bake on the top rack.

Cook for 35 to 40 minutes, until the vegetables are very soft, depending on the size of your vegetables.

Keep refrigerated for up to 6 days. Any leftovers can be eaten on their own, in salads, or paired with cooked whole-grain pasta.

Options for Low FODMAP Diets:

Mannitols and fructans are moderate in fennel. Low FODMAP is defined as less than 1/2 cup.

PLANT POINTS: 5

Stir-Fry with Back Pockets

Here, simplicity triumphs. This stir-fry is designed for Week 1, but it's versatile enough to be mixed and matched with other vegetables after that. We're serving this over quinoa, a pseudo-grain with 8 grams of protein and 5 grams of fiber per cup, instead of a typical protein source. Later in the week, have the leftovers at lunch.

It serves 4 people

A third of a cup of tamari

A quarter cup of rice wine vinegar

2 tablespoons sesame oil, roasted

2 tbsp cornstarch or arrowroot powder

1/4 cup **Broth from a Biome**(optional) or water

2 tblsp. ginger (freshly grated)

1 seeded and minced red chile (optional)

4 scallions, cut (just the green bits)

2 cups chopped broccoli florets only

4 carrots, cut diagonally

1 sliced red bell pepper

2 cups sliced bok choy (leaves and stems removed)

8 oz. sliced oyster mushrooms

4 cups cooked quinoa (serving size)

WHISK TOGETHER THE tamari, vinegar, sesame oil, and cornstarch in a small bowl until smooth. Remove from the equation.

In a large skillet or wok, heat the broth over medium-high heat. Add the ginger, chili, and chopped scallions, if using. Cook, stirring frequently, for 1 minute, or until aromatic.

Cook, stirring frequently, for 5 to 7 minutes, until the broccoli, carrots, bell pepper, and bok choy stems are vivid in color and somewhat soft. Stir together the bok choy leaves and oyster mushrooms for 30 seconds.

In a wok, add the tamari mixture. Cook until the sauce has thickened and the veggies are cooked through, stirring frequently.

Serve over quinoa that has been cooked.

Low FODMAP Alternative:

Add 1 or 2 minced garlic cloves to the tamari mixture after Week 2.

PLANT POINTS: 7

Bok Choy Curry Tofu

This easy supper includes two of our favorite plant-based foods: tofu and bok choy, which are both high in calcium and iron. Baby bok choy is more sensitive than larger bok choy, so choose that if you prefer a milder veggie.

It serves 2 people.

$1^{1/4}$ cups plus 2 tablespoons vegetable broth or **Broth from a Biome**, plus more liquid as needed

1/2 cup coconut milk from a can

1 tablespoon curry powder, yellow

1 tblsp garam masala (garam masala powder)

2 thinly sliced onions (green portions only)

1 tbsp ginger (freshly grated)

1 tblsp. soy sauce

3 cups bok choy, separated leaves and stems

3 oz. bamboo shoots, canned (rinsed)

7 oz. pressed and sliced firm tofu **(Bowls of Tofu Scramble)**

1 teaspoon sesame oil, roasted

Serving size: $1^{1/4}$ cup cooked brown rice

$1^{1/4}$ cup vegetable broth, coconut milk, yellow curry powder, and garam masala, whisked together in a medium bowl until the spices are well blended together.

Remove from the equation.

In a large skillet or wok, boil the remaining 2 tablespoons broth over medium high heat until it shimmers. Combine the scallions, ginger, and tamari in a mixing bowl. Stir for about 1 minute, or until the ginger is mostly broken down and the combination is fragrant.

Sauté for about 5 minutes, until the bok choy stems and bamboo shoots are softened. Add a splash or two of broth if you need more liquid. Set aside the tofu after tossing it with sesame oil. Stir for 30 seconds to mix the bok choy and bamboo shoots into the wok.

Reduce the heat to medium-low and add the remaining bok choy leaves, along with the coconut milk mixture. Reduce the heat to low and cover. Allow to simmer for about 10 minutes, or until the sauce has thickened and the vegetables are soft. Serve over rice that has been cooked.

Make-Ahead Suggestions:

Prior to cooking, chop the onions and bok choy. Refrigerate in an airtight container. This entire dish can be prepared ahead of time, cooled, and stored in an airtight container in the refrigerator, then reheated when ready to serve.

Options for Low FODMAP Diets:

Make sure your curry powder and garam masala don't contain garlic or onion by reading the ingredient label.

It's been boosted!

Chopped cilantro, sesame seeds, and/or bean sprouts can be sprinkled on top.

PLANT POINTS: 7

Risotto with Mushrooms

Yes, risotto takes a little longer to prepare than other dinners, but we find that the steady stirring is meditative. Play a podcast I take pleasure in standing over the stove, preparing a warm bowl of delectable, creamy rice. After thirty minutes, you'll have a creamy, luscious risotto dish free of cream, cheese, or butter. Thank you very much!

It serves 4 people.

4 cups FODMAP-friendly vegetable broth or **Broth from a Biome**

2 tablespoons extra virgin olive oil infused with garlic (**see Note**)

8 oz. chopped oyster mushrooms

Salt

Arborio or other short-grain rice ($1^{1/4}$ cups)

1 tablespoon lemon juice, freshly squeezed

A third of a tablespoon of nutritional yeast

For serving, chopped fresh parsley or fresh chives

Warm the veggie broth in a small saucepot over medium heat. Reduce the heat to low to keep the pot warm after it has simmered for a while.

Heat a separate big pot over medium heat while the broth is heating.

1 tablespoon olive oil, heated until barely shimmering, then add the mushrooms and a pinch of salt once the pan is hot. Cook for about 10 minutes, or until the vegetables are soft and browned. Remove the pan from the heat and set it aside.

In the same saucepan, heat the remaining 1 tablespoon of oil and add the rice. Cook for 1 minute, stirring frequently, until lightly toasted. Add the warmed vegetable broth, 12 cup at a time, with a ladle, stirring almost frequently to ensure the rice absorbs all of the liquid. Avoid boiling the mixture, as this will result in gummy risotto; the heat should be kept low to medium, and the mixture should be kept at a mild simmer.

Continue to add 12 cup of vegetable broth at a time, stirring to mix each addition until the liquid is mostly absorbed before adding more. Until the rice is al dente, the entire process should take about 20 minutes.

Stir in the lemon juice, nutritional yeast, and the mushrooms that were set aside. You may not need any additional salt depending on your broth, but season to taste. If desired, garnish with chopped parsley or chives.

Garlic-Infused Extra Virgin Olive Oil

Note: Garlic should be avoided when eating low FODMAP because it contains a lot of fructans. Because fructans are not lipid soluble, they will not leach into the oil, garlic-infused olive oil is suitable for a low FODMAP diet. Just make sure you don't eat the garlic and only eat the oil. You may buy Fody Foods' garlic-infused olive oil or make your own. To break the skin of a few garlic cloves, crush them; 5 to 6 garlic cloves will require around 1 cup of olive oil. Allow the oil to cool after gently heating it with the garlic over low to medium heat for a few minutes. Remove the garlic cloves and place the oil in the refrigerator.

Options for Low FODMAP Diets:

Try Fody Foods, Savory Choice, or Casa de Santé for a low FODMAP vegetable broth from the grocery.

PLANT POINTS: 5

Parmesan Pepitas

1/2 cup almonds, sliced (20 whole almonds)

1/4 cup pepitas (raw)

A third of a tablespoon of nutritional yeast

1 teaspoon kosher salt

In the bowl of a food processor, combine the almonds, pepitas, nutritional yeast, and salt; process until a fine powder forms, being careful not to turn it into almond butter. Keep refrigerated for up to 2 weeks or frozen for up to 6 months.

Slivered almonds are strong in GOS, making them a low FODMAP option. Reduce the number of nuts to ten.

HARISSA STYLE SWEET POTATO BAR

It serves 4 people.

4 big scraped sweet potatoes

chickpeas from a 15-ounce can, washed and drained

2 tablespoons tahini

2–3 tablespoons harissa paste, depending on personal preference

2 to 3 tablespoons lime juice, freshly squeezed

A sprinkling of olive oil (optional)

Topping: fresh cilantro (optional)

1. Preheat the oven to 400 degrees Fahrenheit. Prick a few holes in the potatoes with the tines of a fork and set on a rimmed baking sheet in the oven. Cook, stirring occasionally, for 45 to 50 minutes, or until the potatoes are just soft.

2. Combine the chickpeas, tahini, harissa paste, and lime juice in a small bowl while the potatoes are cooking. Mash some of the chickpeas into the tahini with a fork.

3. Take the sweet potatoes out of the oven, cut them open, and scoop out about half of the filling. Fill the sweet potatoes with the filling, toss it in, and then return it to the chickpea mixture.

4. Drizzle with a little olive oil if desired, then return to the oven for another 5 to 10 minutes, or until warmed through. Remove from the oven and top with fresh cilantro, if preferred.

PLANT POINTS: 6

CRISPY CHICKPEAS WITH SWEET POTATO BAR

It serves 4 people.

4 big scraped sweet potatoes

4 cups kale leaves, torn

chickpeas from a 15-ounce can, washed and drained

1–2 teaspoons extra virgin olive oil

1/4 teaspoon cumin powder

1/4 teaspoon paprika (smoked)

2 tablespoons tahini

2 tablespoons lemon juice (plus more to taste)

1/4 teaspoon red pepper flakes (optional), plus salt and pepper to taste

1/4 cup flat-leaf parsley, freshly chopped

To taste, season with salt and freshly ground pepper.

1. PREHEAT THE OVEN to 400 degrees Fahrenheit. Prick a few holes in the potatoes with the tines of a fork and set on a rimmed baking sheet in the oven. Cook, stirring occasionally, for 45 to 50 minutes, or until the potatoes are just soft.

2. Toss the greens and chickpeas with the olive oil in a large mixing dish. Rub the cumin and paprika into the greens and beans with your hands to coat them. Bake for 10 minutes, or until the kale is crispy, in a single layer on a baking

sheet. Remove the parsley and return it to the bowl with the tahini, lemon juice, red pepper flakes, if using, and tahini. Season with salt and pepper to taste.

3. Peel the potatoes and cut them in half lengthwise, being careful not to cut all the way through. Massage the potato's skin to fluff the inside, season with salt and pepper, then top with the fried chickpea and kale combination.

PLANT POINTS: 4

SNACKS, DESSERTS, AND DRINKS

Tea with Lemon and Ginger

A s an after-dinner drink, we enjoy this lemon-ginger tea. Ginger improves digestion, and lemon has just the right amount of tartness to fulfill any dessert desires. Feel free to drink as much as you want whenever it suits you.

It serves 2 people.

1 small knob of ginger, cut into four 1-inch slices

1 huge lemon's juice

As desired, 100 percent maple syrup or stevia

Simmer 4 cups water and the ginger in a medium saucepan for 10 to 15 minutes, or more, depending on how strong you like your tea.

Take the pan off the heat and add the lemon juice. Remove the ginger with a strainer and divide the tea between two big glasses. Serve with a drizzle of maple syrup.

To serve chilled, prepare as follows: Add the lemon juice and maple syrup to taste after pouring the ginger-water combination over 4 cups of ice.

PLANT POINTS: 2

Dip in Muhammara

Muhammara is a hot pepper dip with Syrian roots, made with roasted red peppers, walnuts, cumin, and red pepper flakes. This smokey spread goes great with vegetables and toasted sourdough, and it's also great in our **Sandwich with Muhammara.**

Approximately $2^{1/2}$ cup dip

6 red bell peppers, big

1 cup chopped raw walnuts

2 tablespoons extra virgin olive oil

1/4 cup lemon juice, freshly squeezed

1/4 cup balsamic vinaigrette

1 teaspoon cumin powder

1 teaspoon salt, plus additional salt to taste

1/2 teaspoon red pepper flakes, crushed (or more, for a spicy dip)

Preheat the oven to 450 degrees Fahrenheit.

Roast the whole bell peppers on a rimmed baking sheet for 25 minutes, turning after 15 minutes, until lightly browned on both sides.

Place the peppers in a large mixing bowl and cover with a kitchen towel for at least 10 minutes to allow them to steam. This will soften the skin, making it easier to remove.

Remove the skin, core, and seeds after they have cooled. Set aside after rough chopping.

Add the walnuts, olive oil, lemon juice, vinegar, cumin, salt, and red pepper flakes to the food processor's base. To blend, pulse 8 to 10 times. Pulse a few more times to incorporate the roasted peppers. You may make a creamy hummus-like spread or a chunky nut spread out of this. Taste and adjust seasonings as needed, adding extra lemon for acidity, chili flakes for spice, balsamic vinegar for depth, and salt for seasoning.

This will stay in the fridge for up to 4 days if covered.

PLANT POINTS: 3

Broth from a Biome

This broth reduces inflammation, feeds your intestines, and is high in antioxidants. For quick prep, we recommend cooking a batch every Sunday in a slow cooker. To make a more powerful soup, add more aromatics, such as onion and garlic, as the weeks go on. Begin with 1 chopped onion and 2 garlic cloves, then add more as needed.

Warm a cup (or two!) of this soup and whisk in a tablespoon of miso paste until dissolved for a quick snack. Add cubed tofu, chopped onions, roasted mushrooms, and/or cooked kale to make it more filling.

Makes approximately 8 cups

1 large dried kombu piece

1 cup carrots, chopped

1 cup celery, chopped

1 teaspoon mushroom powder or 1/3 cup dry shiitake mushrooms

1 inch of sliced fresh ginger

a teaspoon of nutritious yeast

2 tablespoons extra virgin olive oil

3 tblsp. soy sauce

1/4 teaspoon turmeric powder

Sipper of Miso Biome

Biome Broth (two cups)

2 teaspoons ginger (freshly grated)

miso paste, 2 tblsp.

In a slow cooker, combine the kombu, carrots, celery, mushrooms, ginger, nutritional yeast, olive oil, tamari, turmeric, and 8 cups water. Simmer for at least 6 hours on low. Alternatively, throw in a large stockpot and cook, stirring periodically, for at least 2 hours on low.

Allow it cool completely before straining through a fine-mesh strainer. Divide the mixture into glass containers and store some in the freezer for later in the week and some in the fridge for now. If freezing in a glass container, be sure there is enough area for the liquid to expand. Otherwise, the glass may break!

Warm the broth over medium heat, then remove from the heat and mix in the ginger and miso paste until completely dissolved, about 30 seconds. Pour into two mugs and enjoy.

It's been boosted!

As the broth warms, add 1/2 teaspoon mushroom powder to the biome sipper.

Scatter sliced scallion greens on top.

PLANT POINTS: 6

Oat Balls with Coconut

A pproximately 14 balls (depending on size).

1 cup old-fashioned oats, plus additional oats as needed

1/3 cup coconut flakes (unsweetened)

A third of a cup of peanut butter, plus more if necessary

2 tblsp. maple syrup (100%)

chia seeds (2 tblsp.)

1 teaspoon extract de vanille

1/4 teaspoon cinnamon powder

1 ounce dark chocolate, finely chopped

In the base of a food processor, pulse the oats, coconut flakes, peanut butter, maple syrup, chia seeds, vanilla, and cinnamon 10 to 12 times, until just mixed (you can also just mix these ingredients together in a large mixing bowl until thoroughly combined). Add more oats if the mixture is too sticky to roll into balls. Add more peanut butter if it's too dry.

Pulse in the dark chocolate until it is barely combined.

Using a spoon or a small cookie scoop, pinch off a 1-tablespoon ball. Continue with the rest of the mixture after rolling it into a ball. Refrigerate for up to 3 months or store in an airtight container for up to 1 week.

Notes on FODMAP: While all of the components are low in FODMAP, limit yourself to two balls per serving.

PLANT POINTS: 4

Chia Pudding with Lemon Zest

This Fiber Fueled lemon chia pudding is a twist on lemon pudding. When you have chia seeds, you don't need dairy or egg yolks. When chia seeds are combined with liquid, they expand, resulting in a thick, creamy pudding made with lemon juice and almond milk. After Week 3, add canned coconut milk for a creamier pudding.

Approximately 2 cups

1 cup almond milk (unsweetened)

1 teaspoon lemon zest (freshly grated)

1/4 cup lemon juice, freshly squeezed

1 to 2 teaspoons maple syrup (100%)

1/4 teaspoon turmeric powder

a pinch of salt

chia seeds (1/4 cup)

Whisk together the almond milk, lemon zest, lemon juice, maple syrup, turmeric, and salt in a medium mixing basin. Place in the fridge for 15 minutes after adding the chia seeds and whisking until fully blended. Remove from the fridge, whisk together again, then cover and chill for at least 2 hours, or overnight.

Refrigerate for up to 7 days if stored in an airtight container.

Make-Ahead Tip: Chia pudding can be made ahead of time. It will keep in the fridge for up to a week.

It's been boosted!

PLANT POINTS: 3

Coconut Whipped Cream

It serves 4 people

1 full-fat can of coconut milk (or coconut cream) refrigerated overnight

Carefully open the can and scoop out the solidified coconut on the top half. If you're going to use coconut milk, make sure you just acquire the solid coconut and not the water underneath. You can either throw away the water or use it in another recipe.

You'll use the entire can of coconut cream if you're using it.

Using a hand mixer or a stand mixer, beat the hardened coconut until it is creamy.

PLANT POINTS: 1

TEA WITH DIGESTIVE BLISS

1 person

This is the holy grail of teas for digestion! Here, the gut's superhero herbs come together to form the ultimate squad. Make this recipe your own by modifying it as needed. Peppermint, for example, can aggravate acid reflux, so if you're worried about that, leave it out.

1 teaspoon peppermint leaves, dried

1 teaspoon chamomile flowers, dried

1/2 teaspoon fennel seeds, lightly crushed

fresh ginger slices, three or four 1/4-inch thick pieces

If you have a fresh lemon, slice it.

8 oz. freshly boiled water

Sweetening agent (optional)

Place the peppermint, chamomile, fennel, ginger, and lemon in a small teapot or big mug and cover with boiling water. Steep for 10 minutes, covered. Return the contents of the mug to the mug to sip and enjoy.

Sweeten to taste.

PRO TIP: You may use fresh or dried ginger to make this dish (not powder). If you're using dried ginger, cut the amount down to 1 to 2 tablespoons.

TEA WITH PEPPERMINT

1 person

Peppermint relaxes the intestines and relieves spasms, which may help with gas, bloating, and indigestion. Peppermint was found to be useful for irritable bowel syndrome symptoms and abdominal pain in a systematic review and meta-analysis of placebo-controlled clinical studies.

1 tablespoon peppermint leaves, dried

12 ounces water that has been brought to a boil

Sweetening agent (optional)

Place the peppermint leaves in a large mug, cover with boiling water (212°F), and steep for 3 to 5 minutes. Using a fine-mesh strainer, strain the mixture.

If desired, sweeten with sugar.

TEA WITH GINGER, TURMERIC, AND LEMON

1 person

This tea aids in the relief of nausea, inflammation, and discomfort. Both ginger and turmeric are made from the rhizome of a plant, which is an underground stem that generates shoots from its sides, similar to a root system. Both include potent phytochemicals: gingerol in ginger and curcumin in turmeric. Both have been found to be advantageous to the gut bacteria on numerous occasions. If desired, sweeten with a little date syrup or maple syrup.

1 teaspoon turmeric powder

1/2 big lemon juice

1 teaspoon freshly grated ginger

1/4 teaspoon black pepper, freshly ground

Sweetening agent (optional)

12 oz. boiling water

Whisk together the turmeric, lemon juice, ginger, pepper, and sweetener, if using, in a large mug. Whisk in the hot water slowly.

TEA FENNEL

Fennel helps to relieve flatulence and upset stomach, as well as balance diarrhea and constipation and enhance breathing. What's not to appreciate about that?

In India, fennel seeds are customarily chewed after meals. Anethole, which is chemically related to the neurotransmitter dopamine and has a relaxing, antispasm action on the muscles lining the intestines, is the main component of fennel oil seeds. As a result, it's been demonstrated to be effective in the treatment of irritable bowel syndrome cramping.

fennel seeds, 1 tablespoon

12 ounces water that has been brought to a boil

Sweetening agent (optional)

1. Using a mortar and pestle, the back of a spoon, or the flat edge of a wide knife, crush the fennel seeds. You can also use a glass bottle or a rolling pin to gently shatter the seeds.

2. Cover with boiling water (212°F) in a big mug and steep for 3 to 5 minutes. Using a fine-mesh strainer, strain the mixture. If desired, sweeten with sugar.